Success
From Stress

Other Books by Ralph Wilkerson

BEYOND AND BACK
Those who died and lived to tell about it!

ESP OR HSP?
Have you ever sensed that something ominous was about to happen . . . and it did? Now you can explore the fascinating mysteries of the mind and marvel at the revolutionary mind-moving powers of a supernatural seventh sense called HSP.

LONELINESS: THE WORLD'S NUMBER ONE KILLER
What killed Elvis Presley? Why am I so lonely? Can I die of a broken heart? What causes loneliness, and how can it be overcome? This book about one of America's most serious problems offers startling answers!

REDWOODS, PLANTED BY THE LORD
A thrilling study on Christian maturity reveals the fascinating mysteries which lie hidden in the redwoods.

SATELLITES OF THE SPIRIT
The magnetic force of other worlds affects us. This book takes you on an amazing journey through outer space and beyond to discover the security of lasting spiritual values so desperately needed in these troubled times.

Planned Releases

NOW THINKING
Activating your faith

YOUR HEART IS A HOSPITAL
Spiritual therapy

ERASE THE RACE
With incredible insight into prejudice and racism, this intriguing book will offer the astonishing solution to an age-old problem.

Available at your local bookstore

Success From Stress

by Ralph Wilkerson

Melodyland Publishers
P.O. Box 6000
Anaheim, Calif. 92806

Bible quotations are from the King James Version and The Living Bible, copyright 1971 by Tyndale House Publishers, Wheaton, Ill. Used by permission.

First printing—July 1978

Library of Congress Catalog
Card Number: 78-69962

ISBN: 0-918818-08-7

Printed in the United States of America

DEDICATED TO
the Melodyland Thursday prayer groups,
numbering several thousand,
that have encouraged me to
present these practical
concepts of living

Preface

No one is free from stress. Age, occupation, race and geographical location do not exempt one from the tugs of tension. While writing this book, I had opportunity to test every principle in it. I confess they are workable, for I have lost no sleep and have no ulcer.

These practical teachings can enable you to turn your troubles into triumph and your stress into success.

Some of the names in this book have been changed to protect their identity.

Contents

Driven by competition and lost in overwork,
workaholics never know when to quit

1

Stress or Dis-stress?

"I can't stand it anymore!"

A big man who looks like he may have played football in high school, John is the picture of the harried executive—sleeves rolled up, tie loosened at the collar, shirt slightly rumpled, facing a mountain of paper piled high on his desk. A closer look reveals a profile of tension as he battles the torments of worry and overwork.

Furrowing his perspiration-beaded brow in tense agony, John slams tightly-clenched fists on the desk. As the paper mountain tumbles and the pens and pencils scatter away beyond the illumination of the desk lamp, he punctuates the late night darkness with an anguished cry:

"I just can't stand it anymore . . . !"

Sitting quietly in her backyard swing, rocking slowly back and forth, Suzie clutches her doll, lost in a dream-world of playing house and wonderland fantasies. Suddenly a grating voice shocks her back into the present:

"Suzie . . . *Suzie*! Where *are* you? Suzie. . . ." Mom's head pops through the slightly opened back door of the house.

"There you are!" she storms. "You get right back in here and practice your piano lessons!"

Glancing from side to side as if searching for escape, the little girl drops her doll and reluctantly climbs off the swing. She trudges toward the back door, arms hanging limply at her side. Shuffling slowly through the door, she tries to ignore the familiar drone coming from the stern figure of her mother.

"You should be grateful for the chance to play the piano, child. If only I had that opportunity when I was a little girl. . . ."

"You'll have to leave now. We're closing," the librarian smiled.

"Oh, well," Mike muttered quietly. "These overhead lights were beginning to blind me anyway."

Gathering the books scattered over the broad expanse of the library table, he stood to leave but stopped as he felt his mind go suddenly blank.

"Too much reading, I guess. This cramming for finals is for the birds."

Stepping through the library doors, he tensed as a wave of panic surged over him. Clutching his books more tightly as he walked toward the college dorms, he found his thoughts racing to a possible fate the next morning.

Would he pass the finals? Could he possibly flunk out of school? What would his mom and dad say?

Walking briskly now, Mike bounded up the steps of the dorm to his room. As he reached the door, the fleeting thought of cheating flickered across his mind. Could he? He had never done it before.

Entering the room cautiously to avoid disturbing his roommate's slumber, Mike set his books down on the floor quietly and stretched out on the bed.

"Got to quit that school cafeteria job. Not enough time. . . . But where will I get the extra money I need? Mom and Dad already have put out enough cash." With the heavy hand of exhaustion pinning him to the bunk, Mike's mind churned restlessly. "What if I *do* flunk out of school? I've got to get some sleep. Why can't I sleep?"

We Are All Under Stress

Diverse as these individuals are, they share a common experience: the distress of stress. From harried homemaker to bored assembly-line mechanic, corporate executive to company janitor, frayed farmer to groaning grocery clerk, furious freeway driver to hurrying highway patrolman—all are affected by stress. In this day of pressuring deadlines, even those who write books on the subject are feeling the pinch!

Stress is a leading cause of heart trouble, ulcers and cancer. Perhaps it is the underlying killer, more than all the diseases put together. Like an erupting volcano I witnessed in Hawaii some time ago, the world is boiling and seething under tremendous pressures.

Everywhere we look the scars of stress are visible. Apparent in the furrowed brows of worried businessmen, they can also be seen in the haunting eyes of hurrying housewives, weary career women and frazzled mothers. They are reflected in the decisions of goverment officials and in the irritability of frustrated executives. The church, too, has felt the violent pull of tension. Even children are affected. Recently I met a second grader who had ulcers and was suffering hypertension because of anxiety.

But stress has its productive side. Without it, Edison would not have worked those countless hours to light our cities, Michelangelo to produce great works of art or Salk to develop a polio vaccine.

What then is this strange enigma that produces both ulcers and astounding accomplishments? Dr. Hans Selye, a world authority on the subject, says: "Stress is nonspecific response of the body to any demand made upon it. The word 'stress' allegedly came into common English usage . . . as 'distress'. . . . Activity associated with stress may be pleasant or unpleasant; distress is always disagreeable. . . . Stress is not something to be avoided. In fact, . . . it cannot be avoided."[1]

The dictionary defines it as "a physical, chemical or

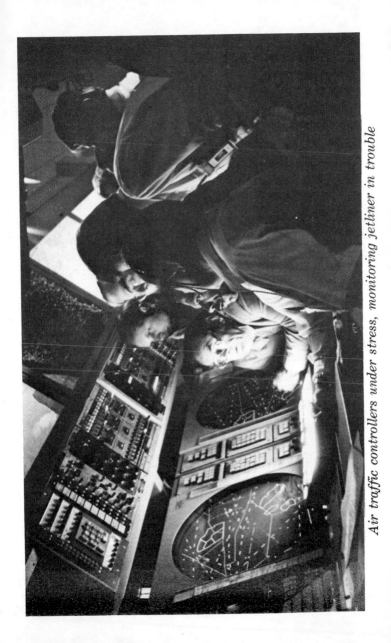

Air traffic controllers under stress, monitoring jetliner in trouble

emotional factor that causes bodily or mental tension," while Dr. Gary Collins, a Christian psychologist and stress authority, says simply that "stress is essentially the wear and tear of living ... each of us experiences ... resulting from the pressures of life.

"When it motivates us to action," Dr. Collins continues, "stress can be good, but when it puts our bodies under prolonged physical and emotional pressure, then the very things that might have been stimulating and fun become destructive and unpleasant instead."[2]

Strain in itself is neither good nor bad, but it's what we make of it that really counts. Now let's take a look at types of tension that struck in Bible days and meet those who mastered the test of their stress.

A Millionaire Mopes

A former millionare, Job sat in the gutter, his rag-draped body full of crusty sores. Penniless, family all but destroyed, Job had to endure the nagging of his wife and the discouraging counsel of his friends to quit in the face of such adversity. Some might say no man could survive this trial. He was enduring more family, social and economic stress in a moment's time than we would expect in a lifetime, yet Job found the strength to endure.

Facing the misery of seeming abandonment by God, this servant of suffering must have felt absolutely helpless. He could do nothing about his situation. Taking a philosophical approach, he moaned,

"Naked came I out of my mother's womb, and naked shall I return. . . ."[3]

His self-pity turned to praise as he pondered the greatness of God. With that shift in attitude, God began to resolve his problems, and his stress slipped away. Once Job conceived the greatness of God, his abundance was restored twice as much as before. That's a real "success from stress" story!

The Paranoid Prophet

Sometimes even greater problems can stem from the pressure of success. Elijah triumphed over the prophets of Baal when he called fire down from Heaven that consumed their pitiful sacrifice. Imagine how he must have felt, virtually sitting on top of the world. Look at the circumstances: Elijah had just seen the enemy defeated in a flaring flash of fireworks. God had vindicated His servant in a sizzle but success turned to stress when Queen Jezebel learned of his triumph and wanted Elijah dead. In panic the prophet fled for his life. Frenzied from exhaustion and hunger, he begged God to take his life.

But God had different plans. Sending a ministering angel to supernaturally feed him and give him water, the sulking seer was enabled to continue on the strength of this sustenance for forty days and nights.

We can learn from this paranoid prophet. There can be a stress from success. The physical reacts on the body, and the body reacts on the spirit. Elijah was drained physically and emotionally, causing him to sag spiritually.

Paul Under Pressure

Beaten, shipwrecked and robbed, the Apostle Paul experienced nearly every kind of stress a person can encounter. Weariness, pain and hunger were frequent hardships. But perhaps his greatest strain was concern for the churches he had established. Compassion kept him in constant prayer for their safety and growth.

How did Paul endure such pressures? He learned the law of transfer—turning his stress over to God. Paul said,

> We are pressed on every side by troubles, but not crushed and broken. We are perplexed because we don't know why things happen as they do, but we don't give up and quit.
>
> We are hunted down, but God never abandons us. We get knocked down, but we get up again and keep going. . . . Yet this short time of distress will result in God's richest blessing upon us forever and ever![4]

Every Christian can follow this example in coping with crisis. If our mission is mandated from Heaven, the battle belongs to God.

No Stranger to Stress

Encountering every experience we meet today, Jesus was no stranger to stress. Rejection was a common trauma in His life. Repudiated by His younger brothers and sisters, misunderstood by his parents and scorned in Nazareth when He began His preaching ministry, Jesus struggled through strain and frustration until ultimate rejection at Calvary.

Physical distress was His constant companion. Jesus felt the chill of nights without shelter, the gnawing pangs of hunger, the parched throat of thirst and the burning blisters of sore feet. Often His heart throbbed with the pain of loneliness—in the wilderness of temptation, under the fire of ridicule, in the agony of Gethsemane, during the intrigue of betrayal, under the scourge of Pilate's whip, at the sound of Peter's denial, while trudging laboriously along the narrow road to Golgotha under His heavy cross and finally suspended in shame above Mount Calvary.

Battling Satan in the sandy desert wasteland, Jesus met the tensions of temptation all of us face and triumphed over the spiritual strains of stress. Mentally and physically drained after fasting forty days and nights, He was tortured by the tempter to eat before the appointed time. Still, He refused to use supernatural powers for selfish gain and continued on to face even greater trials.

Tempted by Satan to demonstrate His divinity by flinging Himself from the Temple, Jesus rebuked the devil for suggesting such a diabolical test. Desperate, Satan attempted one last trial. If only Jesus would fall down and worship him, he promised to give Him the kingdoms of this world without the agony of the cross. Mustering His spiritual strength, Jesus resisted and ordered Satan to get lost.

Fight or Flight

But many are victims of the violent pull of tension. Dr. Collins outlines the physical effects of stress as part of the basic biological "fight-or-flight reaction":

Consider what happens to animals when they are frightened or in other ways under stress. Usually they either run or attack. . . . This has been called 'the fight-or-flight reaction,' and it is not limited to animals. When the stress is great, human beings also have a desire to get out of the way or to fight off the pressure as best they can.

This running or fighting puts an added strain on the body. Because of the effort involved, we must be mobilized physically for the extra action, and this is precisely what happens, *automatically.* Whenever stress comes along, more sugar flows into the blood to give us energy, our senses become more alert, our muscles get tense . . . our whole bodies get geared up. This can be useful when we are in real danger—on a freeway, for example, or facing a sudden crisis which demands all of our skill and alertness.

But what if the stress is more subtle? What if it comes from noisy kids or struggling with a tense home situation? At these times the body still gets aroused physically, but it is inappropriate for us to react by flight or fight. We must control our emotions and clamp down on our reactions. The body therefore begins to fight against itself. It is aroused for action, but the action is squelched.

Naturally, our systems can't take this for long. As a result there may be inner tension, physical disease, or mental breakdown. The body's automatic reaction, which once was a lifesaver for hunters and warriors, has in our age become a crippler and sometimes even a killer.[5]

Most of us are acutely aware of this facet of stress and the anguish it can cause. In today's pressure-cooker culture, we find it all too easy to become steamed up over the little things, each one intensifying the strain which already seems unbearable. Our dis-ease soon develops into the specter of disease as jangled nerves begin to short-circuit, and something has to give.

Broken in spirit, Fred Davis
finds distress behind each door

2

Disease and Dis-ease

With slow, steady footsteps, Fred Davis trudged up the sidewalk to his home. Returning from his custodian's job at William Manning High School,[1] he needed a quick bite to eat and a look at the evening news before he went off again to work at another high school across town. The weekend would be devoted to his part-time business of waxing floors in a few small offices.

Reaching the doorstep of his neatly-kept home, Fred knitted his eyebrows under furrowed forehead, eyes squinting in pain.

"Oh, here go those headaches again," he winced. "When will they go away?"

Glancing to his left at a small clump of bushes, he

muttered, "Billy's forgotten to rake up those leaves again. That boy has no sense of responsibility!"

A rising anger tightened in his throat. Stopping for a moment, hand outstretched for the doorknob, he forced the anger back down into the pit of his stomach. Firmly clasping the knob, he turned it slowly and pushed open the front door.

From the entry way, Fred took a moment to survey the clean, comfortably-furnished house of which he was so proud. Clean, that is, with the exception of his daughter Janie's newspaper clippings scattered all over the living room carpet. Seated amid her mess, Janie looked up and smiled a greeting, but Fred noticed only the clippings. His state of mind changed visibly as he stood there, from fatigue to depression to livid agitation. Kicking newspapers in all directions, he bulldozed through the living room toward the kitchen.

"Daddy!" Janie wailed, "Don't step all over my clippings! I have to share current events tomorrow in history class!"

"Don't you yell at me, young lady!" Fred whirled and snapped. "This house is a pigsty, thanks to you. And your brother is always messing it up, too. I can never come home to a decent house!"

Turning again, he stomped into the kitchen, where his wife Darla busily peeled carrots over the kitchen sink. Pointing toward the living room, he fumed, "Is this the thanks I get for working like a slave to pay off the mortgage on this place and support the family?"

Brushing a strand of errant hair out of her eyes with a forearm, she grimaced. "Don't you use that tone of voice with me!" she snapped. "I work hard all day, too, you know. And this house is not a pigsty; it's neat as a pin, and you know it!"

"Oh yeah?" Fred yelled. He was about to launch another tirade when Darla interrupted.

"Yeah!" she spat. Dropping the knife clattering into the sink, she grabbed a towel from the rack and turned to face Fred squarely. "Listen, you! You don't *have* to work like a slave all week. You could have time to relax if you wanted it. And be better off, too!"

"Well, howd'ya think you'd get all the things you want if I *didn't* work. . .?"

Suddenly, Fred doubled over, clutching his head in agony. Darla's stern expression changed to fright.

"Honey, what's the matter? What's wrong with you? This has been happening much too often. You should quit that night job. I just don't know what you're trying to prove."

As Darla spoke, she took Fred gently by the shoulders, but he wrenched violently away.

"I don't need your sympathy *or* advice! Why do you think I work so much? It's to get away from you and these lazy kids of mine. . . ."

Both of them froze, stunned by his sudden confession. Slowly, Fred turned in disgust and walked aimlessly into the living room. Janie, who had quietly observed the whole scene, avoided looking at him, but he wasn't seeking a glance from her. Staring straight ahead, he shuffled to an armchair and slumped down in exhaustion.

"I can't take this any more," he whispered hoarsely. "Just can't stand it. . . ." Voice trailing off, Fred's face froze into a mask, unmoving, without emotion—until ambulance attendants arrived to carry him to the hospital.

Failing to Measure Up

Fred Davis experienced what is commonly known as a nervous breakdown. Approaching his fifties, he had a job, family and home. Still he felt inadequate. His feelings drove him in a futile attempt to "prove" himself. Failing to measure up to his former standards in control of his family and physical stamina, he felt a sense of failure in life. Instead of accepting the changes which accompany an aging body as a fact of life, he tried to escape—by overworking.

Irritable from exhaustion and excessively concerned with the material things of life, Fred eventually alienated himself from his wife and children. Pressuring himself into more work to provide more things, he became trapped and consumed in the vicious, endless cycle of workaholism. Finally, he collapsed. The more drastic results of self-imposed pressure are very clear—nervous breakdowns, heart attacks and strokes.

"Dis-tress" can also contribute to many other maladies, including such psychological problems as nervousness, irritability, sleeplessness, the inability to concentrate, and loss of muscle coordination.

Physical ailments, too, often can be attributed to stress, including ulcers, hypertension, migraine headaches, arthritis, even dental problems.

According to Dr. James Lynch, hundreds of recent studies indicate that transient types of emotional stress can have significant effects on the heart, blood vessels and blood chemistry. The major risk factors for heart disease recognized in a major study have now also been linked to emotional pressure.[2]

Searching for Sources

Becoming increasingly aware of the complex relationship between body and emotion, modern medical experts are looking for new answers in the treatment of such diseases as cancer. Studies indicate that in many cases, concentrating on the physical problem is not enough. Seeking the emotional roots of illness, doctors are now being trained to treat their patients as a whole. Using this holistic model, diagnoses not only identify an ailment but possible sources in the strains of life.

Also under the scientific scrutiny of the medical world is the return of maladies considered cured that recur when a patient is confronted by a shocking or prolonged adversity. Various factors such as the death of a son, the infidelity of a daughter, or the burden of long unemployment can reawaken dormant diseases, often leading to death.

During a lecture at the University of Florida, Dr. O. Carl Simonton linked the development of certain illnesses with "the loss of a serious love object, six to eighteen months prior to the diagnoses. This is well documented in several longterm studies that have been done. There are over two hundred articles in the medical literature covering different aspects of the relationship between the emotions and stress to malignancy as well as other very serious diseases. The significant thing about this is that obviously not every one who undergoes a serious loss, such as a loss of a spouse or a child, develops a malignancy or any other serious disease."[3]

Dr. Simonton pointed out that such a loss left a crushing sense of hopelessness and helplessness, which greatly affected the recovery of many patients. Often in spontaneous remission or unexpectedly good responses, the patient goes through a visualizing process, seeing himself as being well. "It might be a spiritual thing, God healing them up and down the whole spectrum," said Dr. Simonton. "But the important thing was what they pictured and the way they saw things. They were very positive, regardless of the source, and their picture was a very positive happening."[4]

Imbedded in the personality like a splinter of wood, certain traits have been identified in cancer patients which may somehow link to their suffering. According to Dr. Simonton, these are: an unwillingness to forgive and holding resentment, a tendency toward self-pity, a poor ability to develop and maintain fulfilling long-term relationships and a very poor self image.

Caused by an inability to handle the pressures of life and maintained by the four factors already mentioned, sickness sometimes seems like a gigantic boulder bouncing and rolling rapidly toward the helpless victim of such ravages as cancer and heart disease. Many simply give up, content to await the imminent crushing blow which will free them from the inner pangs of life's stresses. Yet with the aid of loving families, pastors, doctors and friends, the negative mental "visualizing" processes influencing a patient's personal feelings and his illness can be changed to a positive healing picture.

The knowledge that God loves and ascribes worth to an individual can be communicated by those surrounding him. Bringing a strength-renewing sense of power, such an influence can help free the sufferer from a crushing vice of helplessness, reducing the boulder of fear to a tiny pebble.

Nutritional Pickpocket

Like the world's most deft pickpocket—only many times more subtle—stress steals proteins, vitamins and minerals from the body.

This is done so skillfully that we don't even know something important is missing. When certain symptoms develop, we usually can't trace them back to a specific event.

We ask ourselves, "How could this happen to me?"

The answer is: "Quite easily."

Scientists have long suspected that emotional

stress—anxiety, fear, insecurity or anger—drains nitrogen from the body. (Nitrogen compounds make up protein.)

Nevin S. Scrimshaw and associates at Massachusetts Institute of Technology conducted a research project to learn the truth of the matter. Twenty-six male college students were closely observed and tested under tension. At examination time, their pulse rates shot up, many lost weight, and all of them sustained heavy losses of nitrogen, although they ate the usual amounts of protein-containing foods as before their stress.

Another example of nutritional loss through stress was reported in the Annals of the New York Academy of Science by M. A. Ohlsen. While going through laboratory tests in her doctor's office, a middle-aged woman learned that her son had been wounded in combat. Her nitrogen balance immediately swung from positive to negative. A few days later, she got the joyous news that her son would recover fully. Her doctor tested her again, finding that her nitrogen balance had switched from negative to positive.

Stresses such as physical ailments can lead to bio-chemical stresses, too—silently stealing proteins, vitamins and minerals.

Numerous experiments have demonstrated that a high protein diet, before and after surgery, limits the loss of body protein that usually results from this form of stress. It is well known that undernourished and ill persons frequently die in surgery. They often suffer shock on the operating table, are infection-prone and take a long time to heal.

Many Americans, living a life of tension and anxiety, undermine themselves with a steady diet of junk foods. High octane living cannot be carried on with low octane nourishment. Although a comeback is slowly being made for a natural diet with rich nutritional values, the prevalent fare is junk foods, which cause stress.

Obviously, tension plays a leading role in our society. But sometimes it becomes a scapegoat for problems we bring on ourselves. Let me point out a few common areas of stress. Recognizing the symptoms will help defuse the strain before it builds to the point of explosion.

The Stress of Life

Life itself is stressful as we progress from infancy to death. Each stage of development involves the stress of change, and sometimes the pressure points can build until we are overwhelmed.

A valuable tool used by psychologists is the Stress Quotient chart developed by Dr. Thomas Holmes of the University of Washington.[5] Determining the amount of stress in terms of Life-Change Units (LCUs), the chart is drawn from research on hundreds of people of various ages.

According to Dr. Holmes, if your LCU score totals less than 150 points from events happening to you in the past year, you have only one chance in three of a serious change in health occuring within the next two years. Between 150 and 300, the possibility of your becoming seriously ill is about fifty-fifty. But if your score is above 300 points, watch out! An eighty percent chance exists for a major health problem, which could be anything from disease or accident to surgery or mental illness.

Add your score and see where your Stress Quotient lies:

Life Event	LCU Points
Death of spouse	100
Divorce	73
Marital separation	65
Jail term	63
Death of close family member	63
Personal injury or illness	53
Marriage	50
Fired at work	47
Marital reconciliation	45
Retirement	45
Change in health of family member	44
Pregnancy	40
Sex difficulties	39
Gain of new family member	39
Business readjustment	39
Change in financial state	38
Death of close friend	37
Change to different line of work	36
Change in number of arguments with spouse	35

Mortgage over $10,000.00	31
Foreclosure of mortgage or loan	30
Change in responsibilities at work	29
Son or daughter leaving home	29
Trouble with in-laws	29
Outstanding personal achievement	28
Wife begins or stops work	26
Begin or end school	26
Change in living conditions	25
Revision of personal habits	24
Trouble with boss	23
Change in work hours or condition	20
Change in residence	20
Change in schools	20
Change in recreation	19
Change in church activities	19
Change in social activities	18
Mortgage or loan less than $10,000.00	17
Change in sleeping habits	16
Change in number of family get-togethers	15
Change in eating habits	15
Vacation	13
Christmas	12
Minor violations of the law	11

If your LCU totals more than 300 points, my advice is to prayerfully consider some changes in your lifestyle!

Woes of Overwork

Occupational stress is another widespread problem.

America has produced an abundance of Fred Davises, who become lost in overwork as escapism, whether psychological or financial. Driven by competition, desire for a higher standard of living or attempting to escape home and personal pressures, these work-aholics never know when to quit.

Believing long hours of work is an indication of accomplishment, the workaholic justifies his efforts, unaware of his loss of direction. The solution to any problem, he reasons, is to try harder and work more. In the battle of the budget, his solution is to earn more money, not to cut back on the list of things he wants. If he has family problems, longer working hours will allow him to get away and defend his pious reasons for doing so.[6]

It's true that God requires work as a necessary part of our lives, but it is only that—a part! Overwork leads to distress, which God never intended.

Demands of Perfection

Believe it or not, religion also causes stress. Whether inside or out of the church, the average American feels its impact, far too often expressed as guilt. Insisting on doing his own thing, the religious rebel refuses to heed the nagging inner voice, "But it's wrong!" In reaction, he may become hostile or cynical about religion.

Among Christians, the pressure of not living up to man-made standards of holiness is a source of stress. Many have assumed guilt and burdens that God never placed upon them. Sometimes this preconditioning comes from a strict legalistic church background and not from the Bible. Jesus never expected us to be flawless, but He did demand maturity. The Bible verse "Be ye perfect"[7] refers to maturity, not perfection.

Collective Breakdown

Failure to deal with areas of stress has led modern society almost to the brink of collective nervous breakdown. As Alvin Toffler points out, "It is no accident that so many ordinary people refer to the world as a 'madhouse' or that the theme of insanity has recently become a staple in literature, art, drama and film. . . .

"The assertion that the world has 'gone crazy,' the graffiti slogan that 'reality is a crutch,' the interest in hallucinogenic drugs, the enthusiasm for astrology and the occult, the search for truth in sensation, ecstasy and 'peak experience,' the swing toward extreme subjectivism, the attacks on science, the snowballing belief that reason has failed man, reflect the everyday experience of masses of ordinary people who find they can no longer cope rationally with change."[8]

Hurry and Worry

We all are victims of the struggle against stress. And much of it can be traced to the twin curses of hurry and worry.

Have you ever noticed the anxious faces of people on a busy city street? Many of them look as if they are being pressured to death—and they are! Their expressions point clearly to the curse of hurry—going here and there, running all day long, often not knowing why. Usually they hurry because the time already available has been wasted. People who don't know how to plan their time spend a lifetime playing "catch-up."

Resting in God has great therapeutic value. Most of us are so caught up in the busy whirl of involvement that we neglect our spiritual growth and the peace it offers. Once a little girl was found by her mother sitting at the piano, staring at a piece of sheet music. When asked, "Why aren't you practicing?" the child beamed, "Mommy, I'm practicing the rests!"

In life it is just as important to practice the rests as to play the music. Paradoxically, when we slow down we accomplish much more, with less stress, than running in the rat race of our "hurry-age." God promises that by waiting, we can run and not be weary. The word "wait" is not passive, but means permitting it to happen.

Worry, the other curse, is really the plague of this age. Our tendency is to worry about everything. *But Christians don't have the right to worry!* It destroys the promises of the Bible. It pulls down your health, nullifies your faith, dissolves friendships, kills your effectiveness on the job and ruins your witness. "Be anxious for nothing," the Bible says. The only cause for anxiety is when a person is not in right relationship with God and his fellow man.

Often worry is the result of assuming many things upon ourselves at once. Life is seen as a huge dump truck that has just emptied a full load of sand on our heads. Instead, our lives should resemble an hour-glass, with the sand trickling through one grain at a time.

Today I counseled with a couple whose five year old child had recently been killed when a garbage truck backed over him. Because of grief, stress and loneliness, the father had been unable to return to work. The grandmother of the child also was in an accident and is in intensive care, not expected to live.

I shared with them the hour-glass idea: you solve one problem at a time. You live one day at a time. You get on top of problems before they get on top of you. Time heals, even though the process can be painfully slow. Each day has to get better. Don't expect it to be worse.

Josh Billings once said, "I've had a lot of trouble in my time, but most of it never happened." Jesus said, "Don't be anxious about tomorrow. God will take care of your tomorrow too. Live one day at a time."[9]

All the Time in the World

Jesus was the master over stress and the twin curses of hurry and worry, yet He lived without distress. Allowed three years on Earth to win the world, He must have been the busiest person imaginable. Yet He took time for all the ordinary people who came to Him—children, invalids, tax collectors, fishermen—besides being about His Father's business.

If anyone in the world had reason to feel distressed, it was Jesus. But He mastered His pressures just as He conquered all other human failings. J. B. Phillips writes:

> If there is one thing which should be quite plain to those who accept the revelation of God in Nature and the Bible, it is that He is never in a hurry. Long preparation, careful planning, and slow growth would seem to be the leading characteristics of spiritual life. . . .
>
> It is refreshing and salutary to study the poise and quietness of Christ. His task and responsibility might well have driven a man out of his mind. But He was never in a hurry, never impressed by numbers, never a slave of the clock. He was acting, He said, as He observed God to act—never in a hurry.[10]

Taking time for the meaningful activities of life, especially for quiet prayer and meditation before God, will help you break the cycle of hurry, worry, tension and disease. In a society fallen to pieces, Christians can hold together if we stand firm while God does His work.

One of the most important indications of the last days was called "the cares of life" by Jesus. Disease and "dis-ease" are photographic pictures of modern man in his struggle against stress. A result of worry and tension, depression is a wide-spread form of disease, which Fred Davis identified as an enemy.

3

Freedom From Friction

As Fred Davis' family walked into my office, gloom settled in the room. Silently resisting this spirit of depression, I prayed for wisdom and guidance as we talked.

As Darla, Billy and Janie related their distress, I sensed the spiritual attacks that Fred must have experienced. Now they looked to me for solutions. How could this family be reunited? Could these fragmented relationships, which had been broken when the leader fell, be restored?

"Your life as a family has been seriously out of line," I counseled, going directly to the point. Establishing the responsibilities of each person, we discussed what could be done to heal their relationships.

No Time to Relax

"We were once a happy family," Darla recalled sadly. "We used to go out on picnics. Fred really liked that."

She smiled. "After lunch, full of hot dogs and potato salad, he would stretch out for a fast nap." Billy and Janie grinned at the happy memory.

"Yeah, but then it changed," grumbled Billy. A handsome boy, he was quite a success at college. "I don't know when it happened. Maybe it started when he began to work so much. . . . Oh, I don't know!"

His mother's face flushed with guilt.

"I guess that could be partly my fault," Darla blurted tearfully. "I wanted so many things—a house, cars—and Fred longed for his kids to have a little easier life than he had while growing up."

Billy picked up the thought. "You know, that could be it. He grew up in the Depression and never had *anything*—his family could barely afford food. He started working when he was nine. . . ."

"Yes, this is something we've discussed before, Pastor," Darla interrupted. "The kids and I have always been able to talk, and now with Fred, uh . . . well, sick, it's easier for us to discuss our problems with some openness. He never seemed to have the time for that. . . ." Darla's voice trailed off, and Janie, who had been sitting with folded arms straight back in her chair, blurted:

"Yeah, and he didn't have time for a lot of other things, too!" With that, her body heaved with sobs,

Darla and Billy rising to comfort her. Peering through tears that reflected teenage turmoil, she cried, "You see, he was always in a hurry. I can hardly remember when he wasn't. He never had the time to talk with us. A few months ago Dad started getting really grouchy—irritated at every little thing—and depressed, too. He acted so strange and never was satisfied with what Billy and I did around the house and in school." She glanced at her brother as he continued.

"Yeah, he did 'ride herd' on us a lot. He always was worked up, worrying about the bills. 'Not enough money for this, not enough for that,' he'd mumble to himself. I never really gave it much thought then, but maybe he got nagged at so often about not having enough that it just became too much for him to handle."

Billy shot a glance at his mother. Catching his meaning, she turned her head and quickly looked down, the guilt flushing her face again.

"I did nag Fred a lot," she confessed. "We were having a lot of fights. I guess I wanted too much control of the family—paying the bills, clothing the kids, all that stuff. I was telling Fred constantly that we needed more money to pay the bills. Maybe that's why he seemed driven to overwork. . . ."

For a solid hour, confession after confession began to spill out. Like an onion being peeled away, hurts, troubles, fights and misunderstandings were exposed.

Ending with prayer, I asked God to put in their

hearts a desire to be changed to new attitudes and understanding, making their family a place of peace instead of a coliseum of confusion. I sensed a release in their spirits as tranquility invaded the scene.

"Thank you, Pastor," Darla sniffed. "I think I can speak for all of us. I haven't felt this much peace for a long time. What a relief!"

As they left, I suggested to Darla that she and her children make an appointment with Melodyland's Counseling Clinic. The staff, made up of trained psychologists and psychiatrists, could help them on an on-going basis. "If all of you can get your emotional act together, you can better help Fred when he comes home."

This family smiled in agreement and were on their way.

The Family Shelter

The Davis family problems are by no means uncommon. Examining stress in a family or a nation, one can easily find difficulties similar to those experienced by the Davises.

Unquestionably, a family is sometimes a source of stress, but it also is man's greatest haven from the frustrations and anxieties of the modern world. We draw understanding, support and love from each other. But the pressures on today's families are greater than ever. As mobility increases in our society, some families are almost a generation of gypsies because of so many moves. Because of increasing expectations combined with the exhausting strains of succeeding in urban society, more and more families crack under the pressure. An especially vulnerable institution today, the family unit is a prime target for destruction.

Let's take a moment to look at the family roles and the pressures on each member. Your family *can* resist the squeeze of society and win the struggle against stress if it's based on biblical order.

The Father of the Family

The man's position in the home is a paradoxical one. Expected to be strong at critical moments, possessing knowledge and wisdom, the "head priest" should be loving and understanding. He should project a strong father image for his children to be secure.

Unfortunately, this is not always the case. Take Job, for example. His misfortunes destroyed the order in his family. With his children killed and possessions wiped out, his wife took the prominent role, nagging him to "curse God and die!"

But Job reasserted authority over his wife by replying, "Thou speakest as one of the foolish women speaketh. What? Shall we not receive good at the hand of God, and shall we not receive evil?"

Though Job had lost his position in the world, he assumed head of his family. Unfortunately, many men are not as strong as Job. For a variety of reasons, they become weakened and fall apart.

According to Dr. Robert Page,[1] a working man is under a number of strains. Every day he faces fears such as losing his job, the collapse of his company, and personal financial crises. He worries over marriage problems, mistakes, health, impending retirement, senility and death.

Unemployment is a crippler, the stigma of our society. As anyone who has been out of a job can tell you, the popular notion that unemployed men and women are lazy individuals with little education or skill is false. Many are well-trained and desperately seeking work.

Discouragement, anger and wounded self-esteem are keenly felt by the out-of-work head of the household. If he considers himself a "surplus" person, unwanted by society, a tremendous depression can result.

The news magazines recently carried articles on a big coal strike. A photograph in one publication showed an unemployed coal-truck driver and his wife standing in front of an idle truck. Frustration and sadness were clearly etched on their face. One need not stretch his imagination far to see how paralyzing joblessness can be to a man's ego, destroying his effectiveness as a father, husband, and head of the house.

Despite his economic situation, the man is ordained by God to lead his family. He must never relinquish this position, for he is their "covering" before God and man. Family stress can be reduced when the father makes the final decisions and assumes the consequences. By no means is this a license for absolute

*Unemployment bites into the core of
a person's self worth*

domination. Others in the family also will have good ideas to contribute, but the final decision must rest with the one who has the ultimate authority: the husband.

Wives and Mothers

Women were not biologically, emotionally or spiritually equipped to shoulder the responsibilities placed on men. But modern society often forces unrealistic roles upon them. In many instances a wife has to work to help support the family. With so many women competing for jobs, often a woman is forced to take a man's job.

In a Florida hotel I called for a bellman to help with my luggage. I couldn't believe it when a fragile, five-foot girl knocked at the door, asking, "Where's your baggage."

In no way would I let her lift my heavy cases but placed them on the luggage cart myself.

Women who work outside the home are subjecting themselves to stresses they were never created to handle. A professor of medicine at Cambridge University, Dr. Ivor Mills reports, "In today's society, more and more women are being enticed, cajoled and badgered into trying to achieve more and more—far more than they can possibly cope with." Dr. Mills went on to list insomnia and irritability as symptoms of stress-related illness, often causing hormonal imbalances and infertility.[2]

With the increasing pressures on the family, women at home are under more strain. Some wives have told me they feel like a short order cook, fixing meals throughout the day. With Little League, basketball, and various school or church activities, the children's schedules vary and appetites rage. Some families don't even have dinner together. The father comes home late from work, and the wife serves him a warmed-over dinner. She may have a cup of coffee with him, but the children are playing, studying or off to bed.

For awhile, dining rooms were out of style in homes. Because people were eating at different times, houses were built with family rooms and snack bars. We know one builder who refused to put snack bars in homes to encourage families to sit down together at meal times. Many of our children have been raised on the can opener and fast foods because Mother works and Father holds two jobs.

Don't accuse me of being old fashioned for trying to bring people back to the 1940s. The late forties were some of the best days, for the family unit was very strong. World War II had just ended, and it was great for the family to be reunited again. We made time for each other and had respect for each other. The highlight of the day was sitting down together at the dinner table and just talking about what happened that day. With peace in the country, the values of family life took on a new appreciation. Few could afford expensive art, but most homes had wall plaques of home-spun mottos like "The family that prays together stays together," "Be it ever so humble,

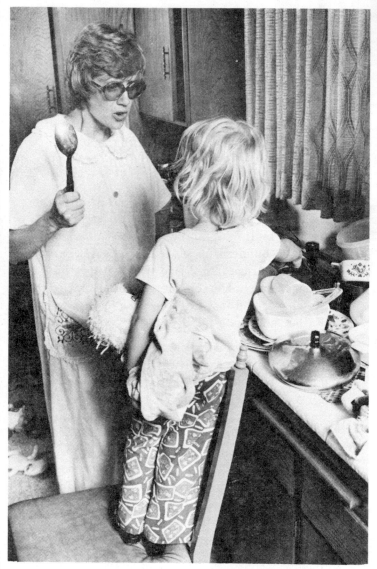

"Can't you see I'm busy?"

there's no place like home," and "Christ is the head of this house, the unseen guest at every meal."

Other favorite pastimes were showing home movies, making home-made ice cream, popping popcorn and pulling taffy. The kitchen was often the center of family activities.

Just this week a leading magazine stated that we have finally finished the cycle and are returning to old-fashioned family togetherness.

The stress of an alcoholic husband or son on drugs greatly intensifies pressures. The whole family suffers economically, socially, emotionally and spiritually.

These anxieties magnify the difficulties of trying to be a wife, mother, housekeeper and sometimes breadwinner, pushing a woman to the breaking point.

Children Cope With Stress

Children are not exempt from the complexities of modern life. Once shielded by the enclosing shelter of the family, they are now on the front lines with the rest of us. Forced to mature early and expected to judge the grey areas of morality which pose difficult challenges even for adults, young people are highly vulnerable.

Alcoholic parents, child-abusers and negligent parents contribute to the tensions children suffer. Perhaps more than ever, the child needs loving understanding to cope with strains unknown to the last generation.

Probably the heaviest areas of stress today are

*Children often feel frustrated
by overdemanding parents*

hereditary. We've come through some of the most tragic years in the history of America—Korea, Vietnam and the era of frustrated flower children, who grew up without experiencing normal family relationships.

At Melodyland we have placed many of these young people in homes to see what a normal home life is like. In our church school, the statistics reveal that a majority of the children come from broken families.

Someone said, "A backward child is one who still has the same parents he started with." That's a Hollywood joke. Our children need parental stability. Many times our girls would run into the house while playing and yell, "Mom! Dad!" All they cared about was the security of knowing we were at home if they needed us. Then they would run outside again and play.

I'm on a crusade to get the family back together. Can't we arrange one time when we can sit down together for meals and talk about pleasant, fun things? Can't we plan our vacations as a family? Surely we can enjoy activities together! Life will be gone before we realize it.

The Future of the Family

In spite of bewildering problems, the family institution will survive. Many families are not only withstanding the attacks on the home but are taking the offensive against the array of perplexing forces. How can your family be a strong refuge, able to resist arising threats?

Consider what God intended the family to be. Larry Christenson writes:

> The family belongs to God. He created it. He determined its inner structure. He appointed for it its purpose and goal. By divine permission, a man and a woman may cooperate with God's purpose and become a part of it. But the home they establish remains His establishment. "Unless the Lord build the house, those who build it labor in vain" (Psalm 68:6).
>
> Thus it is not our marriage, but His marriage; not our home, but His home; not our children, but His children; not our family, but His family. This might sound like pious rhetoric, but it works itself out in thoroughly down-to-earth fashion. If Jesus is truly Lord in your family, it will influence everything from the way you decorate your house to the way you spend your summer vacation.[3]

After taking the proper perspective, strengthen the family by reaching out to each other in love, confessing faults, forgiving one another and healing relationships. Prayer should enter the picture often. Pray constantly for one another and for family needs, whether absent or together. You'll be surprised how much this really helps!

Also I suggest you establish or reaffirm the proper family roles. The most important one is a deep relationship with Jesus Christ. Beyond that, a family needs divine order, as outlined in the Bible:

Wives, submit yourselves unto your own husbands, as unto the Lord. For the husband is the head of the wife, even as Christ is the head of the church: and he is the saviour of the body. Therefore, as the church is subject unto Christ, so let the wives be to their own husbands in everything.

Husbands, love your wives, even as Christ also loved the church, and gave himself for it; that he might sanctify and cleanse it with the washing of water by the word, that he might present it to himself a glorious church, not having spot, or wrinkle or any such thing; but that it should be holy and without blemish. So ought men to love their wives as their own bodies. He that loveth his wife loveth himself. For no man ever yet hated his own flesh; but nourisheth and cherisheth it, even as the Lord the church: for we are members of his body, of his flesh, and of his bones. . . .

Children, obey your parents in the Lord: for this is right. Honor thy father and mother; which is the first commandment with promise; that it may be well with thee, and thou mayest live long on the earth.

And ye fathers, provoke not your children to wrath: but bring them up in the nurture and admonition of the Lord.[4]

This is one of the most striking passages in the Bible! The family is the earthly analogy of Jesus and the church.

Sometimes it's hard to turn your family over to God. But if you have "trained up" your children according to God's order and plan for their lives, you must commit them to Him. His love and investment in them is even greater than yours.

Togetherness in the home is a top priority. There's absolutely no substitute for quality time spent with each other.

Finally, arrange a time for family devotions. If possible, the father should conduct this important time of spiritual communication with his children. It should be structured so simply that even the youngest can participate.

Properly related, the family is a harbor of happiness in a storm-tossed world. Our responsibility is to protect it and develop its potential. The solid family is the base of security from which we can launch into the stress of society—and conquer it.

4

Creativity From Crisis

I waited confidently in the city hall for the final verdict on the zoning change of Melodyland Theatre to a church. Already this had unanimously passed the City Planning Commission. Since it was merely a matter of procedure, I had instructed the congregation not to be concerned about attending this hearing. We had done our homework; everything was in order. We were sure of success.

Suddenly one of the oldest and most respected councilmen, Mr. Smith, opened the door and motioned to me. Leaning down, he whispered, "Reverend, it's bad news. We have a rigged vote. Since three of the councilmen have bars, and Melodyland has the largest bar in Orange County, they have decided to turn you down. There will be no church in a recreation area in Anaheim."

I couldn't believe my ears. Suddenly, my world had fallen apart. The elderly councilman was right; the vote was four to one, rejecting the rezoning.

The few people from the church who were present crowded around me at the door. The newspapers were there, asking, "Now what are you going to do?" One of our church members muttered, "Yeah, Pastor, you have already sold our old building. Now where do we go?"

In that moment an intense resentment gripped me, and I angrily said to her, "We'll fight back. I'll never lose." At that precise second, a news reporter snapped my picture. Can you imagine the embarrassment of seeing my picture in the paper with that fiery look? The caption read: "Pastor says he's a fighter."

When I went home that evening, God impressed upon my thoughts, "Don't you know by now that my specialty is turning stress into success?" He gave me favor with the city attorney. In a few days the official called me in and said, "Reverend, you don't really have a problem. In fact this will work to your advantage. You can have a welfare exemption, for you're doing more welfare work than anyone else."

Today our property is still commercial and what an advantage! Because we can't call Melodyland a church, Protestants and Catholics worship together. Since it still looks like a civic auditorium, non-Christians feel at home.

The principle of creativity from crisis was present in the creation. Earth was in a crisis of chaos. From this, God brought order and restored the planet to perfection. He then looked upon His creation and said, "It is good." Immediately He faced another emergency: who would rule and maintain the new world?

Out of this critical circumstance, God formed an amazing new creature from the dust of the ground and breathed into him the breath of life. Calling him Adam, the Master Designer placed His new creation in a garden called Eden. Before man passed a parade of animals, male and female, which Adam named one by one. But for Adam there was not found a companion. Faced with another emergency, God mused, "It is not good that man should be alone; I will make a helpmeet for him." From this crisis came God's most delicate creation—woman.

Throughout history, man and God have faced many critical turning points. The triumphant entry of Jesus turned into the calamity of the cross. What could be more tragic? Yet out of the cross came the rhapsody of resurrection.

If there's one word that describes what is happening today it's "crisis." Nationally, politically, spiritually, financially and emotionally, crisis best portrays the severity of pressures we all face.

Yet crisis can drive us to creativity. "Necessity is the mother of invention," an old adage goes. Some of our greatest discoveries would never have evolved had not our crises demanded new experiments.

Job's Triumph Over Tension

Have you ever experienced times when one problem piled on top of another, and before you could get those solved still another was added to the heap? This is the kind of situation Job encountered. But he knew how to turn his crises into creativity. Let's examine the types of tensions he endured.

First, *financial pressure.* Job lived with stress. He had everything and lost it. But his attitude enabled him to survive. "Naked came I out of my mother's womb, and naked shall I return thither," he said. "The Lord gave, and the Lord hath taken away: blessed be the name of the Lord."[1]

Is it wrong to be rich? Absolutely not! Many godly men of the Bible were prosperous. God doubled Job's wealth in his later years.

But can you imagine having all this wealth and prosperity one day, and the next it is swept away? I have met people like that. Financial pressure is no sign God doesn't love you. He hasn't turned His back on you. Job had not sinned. The Bible says, "In all this Job sinned not. . . ."[2] Neither did he blame God.

I have seen some who hold God responsible for their financial reverses. But He doesn't send anything but goodness to His children. God permitted Job's distress to bring him into a deeper relationship. His attitude was changed, and this is an important lesson today. Being content with what we have, we can say, "Lord, if that's what you have given to me,

I'm thankful for it. I'm going to see it through. I believe you are going to help me."

Second, *Job had family pressures.* He lost his children, several sons and daughters. They were at a birthday party when suddenly fierce winds blew the house down. All of them were killed at once. Only a servant survived to bring the sad news to Job.

How would that strike you? Not just one child gone, but all your children. Would it seem God was against you? Children can be lost in a variety of ways. Many have strayed in higher education or have drifted into the occult.

I believe we can instruct our children in the ways of Christ until they are so grounded in God's Word they will never lose their faith. One of the wisest men of the Bible said, "Train up a child in the way he should go: and when he is old, he will not depart from it."[3] One never gets away from solid teaching. The only thing that will hold our children today is a firm grip on God's Word.

Job's pressures also affected his marriage relationship. In financial misfortune, his wife remained true. In family sorrow, she was by his side. But when he was covered with boils, she screamed, "Curse God and die!" Fortunately, Job chose to listen to God and overcame his dilemma.

Third, *Job had a friends crisis.* Someone said, "A friend is one who steps in when the world steps out." Yet Job's associates became his critics, mouthing the usual explanations of suffering with pompous self-righteousness that they earned the infamous title of "Job's comforters."

Elihu, a young scholar who thought he had all the answers, argued that suffering disciplines and purifies the soul. The underlying suspicion of Job's comforters was that he must be hiding horrible secret sins for which God was bringing punishment.

Fourth, *Job had a physical crisis.* Immobile with boils covering his body and raging with fever, this patriarch of suffering was in deep misery.

Have you ever been flat on your back and couldn't help yourself? Or so sick you couldn't pray? I have. We talk so much about Job's sickness, we often fail to notice his healing. The Bible says he not only lived to raise a new family, but to enjoy his grandchildren and great-grandchildren. Out of his crisis Job emerged a model of triumphant faith.

Fifth, *Job's biggest problem was a faith crisis.* His faith being severely tried, he lost confidence in himself.

Have you ever felt you just couldn't go on? I have seen men who couldn't find work because they didn't believe in themselves. They had lost their direction. When in balance, ego is important to survival. It is a God-given trait that drives us to solutions.

Purpose in Pressure

We are seeing crisis in our government today. And it's confusing to young people. A teenager asked me one day, "What can I believe in?" But the conflicts within our nation are not an indictment against the American system.

I believe in America. God has made this a great nation because of its founding principles. Never has there been a greater opportunity for spiritual renewal in the nation than now. What if men in high places all over the country would show a renewed dependence upon God?

Revival seldom comes without stimulation from crisis. In Bible days God always intervened in nations when they came to a point of no return.

Denominationalism and traditionalism have forced the church into crisis. A famed bishop recently declared, "There is totally no hope for the church today." But he hasn't been where I've been. God is bringing down barriers and doing a new work by His Spirit among people of all denominations.

Businessmen are nervous and trembling inside because the profit squeeze is so tremendous today. It's hard to succeed, but God has the solution.

A purpose exists for crisis in personal life. The Bible says, "If thou faint in the day of adversity, thy strength is small." The Psalmist said, "Thou hast enlarged me when I was in distress. . . ." The Apostle Paul wrote, "I take pleasure in . . . distress for Christ's sake: for when I am weak, then am I strong."[4]

Said the path to a rose, "What makes you smell so sweet?"

"When I am crushed, it brings out my delicate fragrance," replied the rose.

Escape into alcohol—no chance to profit from crises

"Humph!" snorted the path. "When I'm trampled, I only get harder and harder."

The weights of perplexities and pressures are meant to make us stronger and sturdier. Yet crises affect people in different ways. The situation which stimulates one to great heights of achievement may land another in a mental hospital. Most of us employ various psychological defenses for protection against the strains of life. Confronted with the death of a loved one, for example, one person may turn to God for comfort while another loses touch with reality. In less extreme circumstances, many become so far removed they become immobilized—like Fred Davis.

The "escape from reality" is a common means of coping with stress. Running away from the unpleasant facts of life, the fugitive loses himself in anything that would take his mind off stark reality. Alcoholism and drug-use, overwork and compulsive television viewing are subtle attempts to avoid facing the facts of anxiety and dealing with them effectively.

Pleasure in Pressure

Everyone suffers distress. I want to show you how to turn those pressures into pleasures.

First, *pace yourself.* Identify danger signals before it's too late. We all have different stress levels and should learn where they are.

Dr. Hans Selye discussed this issue during a recent interview. "One striking thing we've discovered is that there are two main types of human beings: 'racehorses', who thrive on stress and are only happy with a vigorous, fast-paced lifestyle; and 'turtles,' who in order to be happy require peace, quiet, and a generally tranquil environment—something that would frustrate and bore most racehorse types," he said.

"If a danger does exist, its main cause is that some people occasionally mistake their own type and push themselves beyond their normal stress endurance. And that, of course, should be avoided. . . .

"Each of us is really the best judge of himself, and we can gradually develop an instinctive feeling that tells us whether we are running above or below the stress level that suits us best. There are also revealing body clues. Animals in a stressful situation invariably show an increased amount of body movement, as do humans. . . . There are also behavioral indicators, such as insomnia or irritability. Deciding on your own type and detecting when and where you are prone to stress isn't very difficult once you've acquired this knack of being more self-aware. After some years of practice, I now know quite well when I've had enough, and then I stop; I don't need any complex scientific test to help me decide. And then I take steps to protect myself."[5]

Perhaps the greatest philosopher who ever lived, Socrates summed this up in his most famous maxim: "Know thyself." We need direction and goals in our lives, but we must be aware of our limitations. Exceeding these, we run the risk of stress overload, when shredded nerves refuse to carry on any further.

Second, *take time to relax.* Constantly on the go,

many dread the unoccupied hour as much as terminal illness. Relaxation is a vital antidote to the constant daily pressures we face.

A national magazine recently listed several ways to reduce stress, three of which emphasize rest.[6]

1. *Plan some idleness every day.* We schedule everything else in our lives; why not include periods of rest, too? We can follow God's example in this. After six days of intense supernatural creativity, He "rested on the seventh day from all his work. . . ."[7] Jesus once said to His disciples, "Come ye yourself apart into a desert place and rest a while."[8] Many Bible verses emphasize creative idleness.

2. *Have a place for retreat at home.* We all need to be alone, working out problems and unwinding from pressure. Develop a signal with your family that tells them, "Do not disturb."

3. *Plan frequent, leisurely vacations.* You needn't take an expensive trip to have a vacation. Sometimes an overnight stay in the next town is enough. When an excursion is possible, avoid structuring it to the point you can't relax. So what if you "waste" a day of your life? You would squander many more in the hospital from exhaustion or breakdown!

So many people say, "We have children and can't afford expensive vacations." That's true. Traveling can be very costly these days. Yet, simple—even imaginary—trips can be fun.

When we first moved to Anaheim, our neighbors told us one day that they could hardly take a vacation because the father's job demanded a very irregular schedule. My wife, Allene, suggested she outfit the children with a pup tent and simple camping equipment and let the children "camp out" all summer in the backyard at home.

The mother bought the equipment for Christmas that year, telling us later it was the best money they ever spent. The next summer the children played camping in their backyard. Armed with flashlights and sleeping bags, they slept in the tent at night underneath their parents' window. In the daytime they had cookouts and ended their activities with a campfire after dark.

We can relieve our tensions in a variety of other healthy ways. Almost a two billion dollar industry today, hobbies are growing in popularity. Social interaction is another stress reliever. Along with spiritual nurture, I believe part of the church's responsibility is to provide a warm social atmosphere.

Physical fitness is an increasingly popular relaxer. Jogging, bike riding, tennis and racquetball are part of the national obsession with exercise. Our Congressmen in Washington have taken physical activity seriously in an effort to alleviate anxiety and thus do a better job.

The emphasis on exercise indicates a healthy atti-

*Pressure of the match—player
channels stress into proficiency*

tude. God expects us to keep our bodies in good working order, avoiding the buildup of tension caused by inactivity. What a thrill to experience the pressures melting into pleasure after a good workout. You feel ready to tackle the world!

Third, *realize crisis is a channel of creativity*. Just as men of God in the Bible turned trauma into triumph, many today have harnessed the energy produced by the stress of need and directed it into creative channels.

The world's great inventions might have lain hidden had it not been for the urgency of discovery. The force of need creates a stressful tension. This in turn builds demand, which motivates us to function. Any form of creativity—music, writing, building houses—comes when we feel the need to produce. Many fail to realize how much creativity goes into problem-solving.

When I was in South Africa recently, I saw how diamonds are made. Do you know this precious sparkling gem would not exist without the creative force of stress? Are you aware that a pearl is formed by the agitation of a grain of sand and that oil cannot flow without pressure? Without the strain of deadlines, writers would not produce, musicians would not compose, and students would not study.

Right at this moment, pressing needs are putting us under pressure. Air pollution is a big problem in Southern California, but because we're attempting to solve it, smog levels have decreased in the past ten years. The energy crisis is forcing us to find new sources of power. The race for space brought us tremendous techniques and incredible inventions which we use in all walks of life—medicine, transportation and industry.

Fourth, *concentrate on one task at a time.* I know people who look at their schedule for the next few months and recoil in horror. Telescoping the future, they compress all their responsibilities into one overwhelming heap. Instead, focus on one problem at a time. Just as a book is written page by page, live your life one day at a time. Jesus counseled, "Leave tomorrow's troubles for tomorrow!"[9]

Fifth, *avoid people who are irritable.* We often reflect the attitudes and emotions of those around us. Just as peaceful people bring calm to a situation, over-competitive and abrasive associates can set us on edge.

Finally, *schedule yourself.* Get up earlier so you don't have to hurry. Take a leisurely shower, and have a good breakfast. Leave for work in plenty of time to drive safely.

Usually when I start for the office, I have a handful of tapes to listen to. Some are Bible reading; others are sermons. Often people wish to tell me something when I don't have time to listen in depth.

"Do you have a tape recorder?" I'll ask. "Would you mind putting it on tape so I may listen later?"

I have forty minutes to drive on the freeway. While other motorists are fighting traffic, I'm making use of my time. I may listen to a tape, catch five minutes of the news or pray. In any event I'm excited by the time Melodyland comes into view, ready for new challenges and fresh opportunities.

A Philosophy for Pressure

Dr. Selye has his own recipe for coping with pressure:

"The first ingredient . . . is to seek your own stress level, to decide whether you are a racehorse or a turtle and to live your life accordingly.

"The second is to choose your goals and make sure they're really your own and not imposed on you by an overhelpful mother or teacher. . . . I've seen too many cases of doctors who really wanted to be musicians, or office clerks who really wanted to be plumbers or carpenters, not to realize how much stress is caused and suffering is involved in trying to live out choices other people have made for you.

"And the third ingredient to this recipe is altruistic egoism—looking out for oneself by being necessary to others, and thus earning their goodwill. I've always advised my children and students not to worry about saving money or about climbing the next rung on their career ladder. Much more important, they should work at making sure they're useful, by acquiring as much competence in their chosen fields as they can—their ultimate protection no matter what the future holds in store."[10]

Dr. Selye's philosophy is good as far as it goes, but it dead-ends in self. While earning the love of others through service is a practical way to overcome stress for the future, such a limited and self-serving objective forces the individual inward, stunting growth. It also leads to pressure reflected in these nagging questions: "Am I really useful? Couldn't they get along without me? What if I'm sick?"

The Spiritual Solution

We have another creative means of dealing with stress, one that goes beyond the physical and psychological approach. God offers the spiritual solution which, combined with some of the human techniques that have been mentioned, will bring a satisfying release from the tensions of life.

Psychologists say we experience anxiety as part of life, a vague uneasiness that derives from being aware of our mortality and the dizziness of our moral freedom.[11] Manifested in a number of ways, anxiety can be traced to man's separation from God. No amount of therapy or mental exercise will remove this tension because only God can bridge the chasm between Him and us.

In Jesus Christ this space has been spanned, making us victorious in the struggle against stress.[12] Jesus promises us His peace, which no human can understand.[13] It must be experienced, not analyzed.

When our fellowship with God is restored, we are free to unload the weight of our burdens on Him. Then we can be quiet before Him in perfect peace, for "quietness and confidence shall be your strength."[14]

Jesus told us to be anxious for nothing.[15] Because

He has never issued an order without supplying the power to perform, He must have given us the ability to carry out this command. Our task is to take Him at His word. Anxiety has no place in the kingdom of God, which is composed of "righteousness, peace and joy in the Holy Spirit."[16]

This supernaturally-sustained liberty is the only real freedom from stress. Delivered from the bondage of dis-stress, worry and failure, we are at peace with God and our fellow man. Hearts flooded with tranquility which nothing can disturb, we are filled with the ultimate source of creativity, ready to go through life with a balance between work and play. With God's help, we can turn crisis into creativity and fully enjoy our moments of leisure.

5

Living Leisurely

Almost unnoticed, leisure has become America's number one industry. Major-league baseball draws more than thirty million fans. At least one hundred million are involved in swimming sports. Tennis is up forty-five percent in the past three years, while movies attracted more than a billion viewers.[1]

Still, many are like the man who confessed, "I build bird feeders for everybody in the neighborhood on weekends. I hate it, but it keeps me busy!"[2]

Never before have we had so much free time or such difficulty filling it. According to leisure expert Dr. Alexander Reid Martin, "We have had to adapt to an unforeseen world which has completely reversed itself; now life off the job and not life on the job predominates to an enormous extent. This abrupt change caught us completely unprepared."[3]

The Weight of Work

Not knowing where to go or what to do with their time, most people face the weekend feeling the weight of work. Instead of sleeping in the hammock, sunning at the beach, hiking in the mountains or relaxing in the backyard pool, millions of Americans exhaust themselves trying to catch up on the household chores. The weekend slips by unnoticed, and the worker sleepily faces Monday morning wondering why he's so tired.

Drilled into us as children, the virtue of hard work becomes an ingrained part of our personality. Although creativity grows out of leisure, we feel vaguely uncomfortable when facing unstructured hours. Dwight Rettie, executive director of the National Park and Recreation Association, explains:

Now the American society, as well as others, is going through a period of profound change. We seem to be wandering in a kind of no-man's land between the age of technology and whatever it is that shall replace it—what some have labeled the post-industrial society. The old work ethic is becoming frayed. Too many workers have noted that their individual efforts do not make much difference to the system. They are less able to define what they do, let alone its value, less able to find fulfillment and satisfaction in ordinary employment.[4]

Out of this confusion staggers the weary worker. With time off, he must find more work to make ends meet. His alternative is to flop in front of the television set, bored and lacking money for other activities he could enjoy.

More leisure, fewer ideas on how to spend it and over-crowded recreational facilities add up to immobilized frustration. Today's lack of direction and purpose extends to nearly everyone's spare time, haunting them with the specter of stress when they should be relaxing.

Resurgence of Recreation

Although affecting millions, this dilemma happily is not the plight of all. A growing number of Americans *do* know how to spend their leisure. They make practical plans for vacations and stick to them, enjoy inexpensive yet fulfilling hobbies and generally know how to make the most of their time off.

"Americans are developing a leisure mentality," says Elizabeth R. Owen, a recreation analyst for the U.S. Department of Commerce, "and that is powering an expansion in buying that's growing in some areas by twenty percent a year."[5]

Where are Americans spending these hard-earned dollars? The national trend is toward the "old-fashioned pleasures" of physical fitness, the arts and education. Interest in recreation and leisure has become so great that educational institutions across the U.S. are offering courses of study to prepare men and women for careers in park and recreational management and for teaching such hobbies as ceramics, dance, sculpture, writing and music. Many are quitting their old jobs and starting new careers, often expanding hobbies into full-time occupations.

America is on an amusement craze. Disneyland's fantastic attractions draw thousands each day. On warm, sunny days, beaches are overloaded. Recreational parks are crowded. Because we don't have enough room to handle the people who want to play, having fun becomes stressful.

Well-balanced and happy, those who can afford popular amusements seem to be coping well with life, compensating for excess stress by relaxing recreation. But what about the others?

Don't Do Things You Don't Want to Do

Constantly standing on the battle lines of stress, they must keep going to survive economically. Having little time for leisure, they face the continuing dilemma of distress. Many work at unpleasant jobs to afford the enjoyable things in life. But how many are trapped with pay so low they can't enjoy life on their days off?

Stress is *making* yourself do the things you don't want to do, then doing them *when* you don't want to. Life becomes monotonous when we do the same thing over and over again.

An amusing incident occurred one day when our

*Fun with the family can
take the mind off weekday woes*

nephew went shopping with the ladies. Allene tells it this way:

We were buying dress material in San Francisco once when Freddy was four years old, so we thought it would be fun to take him along.

We went from department store to department store examining bolts of cloth. He was so little and couldn't understand why we kept looking at all that material. So we said, "We have one more stop to make, Freddy. The White House. Then we'll go to lunch."

"Oh, boy! The White House, the White House!" he squealed, thinking at least it wouldn't be another store.

As soon as we got off the escalator to the material department, Freddy looked puzzled. "Is *this* the White House?" he asked, apprehensively peering over a counter.

"Yes," I replied quickly, examining another bolt.

"Well this is where we were a while ago," he whined, because it was another material department.

Leisure is sometimes like a merry-go-round. We get off the same place we got on, feeling confused like Freddy.

We had a large lawn at our last home. It was almost an acre, and I decided—like a good husband—to exercise for my health and economize. Visiting a major department store, I found a tractor lawnmower to cut down the hours.

It was a lot of fun putting the machine together, and mowing was quite enjoyable until I turned over two times on the steep hill, narrowly missing getting severely cut by the whirling blade.

Usually I would get about five telephone calls while I mowed the lawns. Rushing into the house to answer the phone, I'd honor Allene's request and take off my shoes. But invariably, the grass cuttings in the cuffs of my trousers would form a trail through the house. Of course she'd scream, "Ralph, I just vacuumed the floor!" Added to this were the frustrations of repairing the sprinkler system every time I broke a head and the pruning and weeding which I thoroughly detested.

Sometimes we were expecting company, and I would come in hot and smelly from the yard in a rush to get my bath and change clothes. One day while going through all this routine, I said, "Lord, I *hate* this. Why am I doing it? How much is my time worth?"

My philosophy is this: don't do anything that you do not enjoy—unless you must. Does this mean you shouldn't work if you dislike your job? No. Find work you enjoy.

I decided to quit mowing that lawn and hired my neighbor—a college student—to do it.

Another time while mowing the grass I mopped my brow and sighed, "Lord, you know I have too much lawn. I wish you'd help me here."

His answer came about a month later, but not the way I expected. We were on a round-the-world evangelism tour, and I received a frantic phone call one night in India.

"Oh, Pastor," the worried voice began. "You won't believe it, but half your lawn has just fallen onto the freeway! Your hill is on a slide, and there's a big crevice near your house. . . ."

As the gruesome story unfolded, a thought flashed through my mind: "What am I going to do?"

A result of heavy rains, the slide was making newspaper headlines, and television cameras were beaming the scene to millions of viewers. Suddenly, I realized my prayer had been answered. The house was untouched, and I didn't need that much lawn anyway!

Some of our stress comes from circumstances we could resolve, if we would just not fight against it. We can't resist the current all the time, so we flow with situations.

Have you ever noticed that when something is enjoyable time flies and your tasks become delights? Many needlessly endure duress because they struggle against time. Fighting the clock, they somehow manage to get through another day.

"If I can just make it to five o'clock!" many groan. Then they must plow through congested freeways to face the problems of unpaid bills, uncleaned homes and uncooked meals.

Everytime Allene gets on the freeway she observes different types of people.

"There's the road hog who's always changing lanes, screeching and honking to get by," she laughs. "Then I'll drive by another person who's listening to the radio or a tape. While traffic is standing still, instead of fighting, squirming and twisting his face into a frown, the motorist is smiling or singing along and sipping coffee."

Both kinds of drivers have similar pressures and the same traffic. Both face the same deadline. Each must get to work. But attitude spares one from undue stress.

Waking up in the morning is exciting to me. Looking forward to new challenges and opportunities, I am raring to go, wondering what excitement awaits today.

How to Turn Leisure Into Living

While many are forced into retirement against their wills, most senior citizens look forward to their latter years of leisure with enthusiasm.

Whether anticipated with delight or dread, the routine of retirement usually follows a similar pattern. For years you've had a fast flurry of activity at the office, the price exacted for success. Suddenly one day you realize it's time to retire. Picking up your final check, you say goodbye to friends and walk out with a whoop of joy: "Now I can do what I want!"

For the first two or three weeks, life is exciting.

You go fishing, fix the house, read a bestseller or catch up on all those neglected chores. Then it dawns on you: this is a "permanent" vacation. No job awaits after it's finished. You're in good health, able to work, and yet ...

After awhile, you run out of places to go and challenging activities to fill the now slowly passing days. You have more time on your hands than Timex has watches!

How can this dilemma be avoided?

First, *don't retire abruptly.* Take on some additional responsibilites. One need not drop out of life because his career draws to a close. With proper planning, you can prepare for a new occupation unlimited by age.

If you're in good health, why not start your own business, write that book you've always wanted published, or enter fulltime Christian service? Television news commentator Eric Sevareid was taken off the air by his network's mandatory retirement policy, causing a minor furor. Now he is doing special documentaries for independent news stations. You can find a meaningful activity and continue to be productive long into your golden years.

Fortunately, the church is beginning to recognize that senior citizens are an untapped reservoir of intelligent, gifted people. With more than two hundred outreach ministries, Melodyland involves many retired persons in work and service—counseling, praying, even envelope stuffing for our huge mailings. The list is almost endless. Retirement need not abruptly end your usefulness.

Second, *invent creative activity.* With a lot of time on their hands, widows and retired women tend to relive their lives through their grown children. Taking on additional problems, anxieties and worries, they increase stress on both sides. They shouldn't sit in a rocking chair all day thinking about their children's problems. Older women can become valuable volunteers in a service organization, hospital, school or church. Knitting, crocheting and needlepoint are but a few practical hobbies to keep them occupied. Creative leisure will reduce much of the stress elderly persons suffer.

Attitude and finding the right activity are keys to a happy retirement. To relieve her stress, Allene likes to work crossword puzzles. But while she's easing her tensions, I'm under a strain because nothing makes me more nervous than to watch someone work a puzzle. To one person an activity may be recreation, to another it could be stress. Attitude is the determining factor.

For me, fishing releases tension. I enjoy watching the rhythmic beat of the waves and playing games of hide and seek with the fish. They hide and I seek, trying to outsmart them. I enjoy fishing because it gives me time to think and create.

Recreation is really "re-creation." It is a change of pattern or pace. Unlike at the office, your attention is focused on a good time, laughing, letting down your hair and enjoying the fun of fellowship.

Retirement doesn't mean you're on a 365-day a year vacation. You have to get up in the morning, make breakfast, clean house, weed the garden, service the car, buy the groceries—the same routines of responsibility we all have. But with the right attitude and a little imagination, you can turn retirement leisure into creative living.

Third, *live simply*. Some people have the mistaken idea they must play all the time. Few have that kind of money. While fishing and golfing are fun, many can't afford the boats nor the green fees to enjoy these activities regularly.

I think the big word in living leisurely is *adjustment*. You have to adjust your time, your finances, your friends and your attitudes. Reading can be the cheapest hobby in the world because the library has thousands of books to choose from. But I know older people who will not read. One day I listened to one woman complain about her loneliness.

"Why don't you read?" I asked.

"I don't like to read," she whined.

"Why don't you get some tapes and listen to them?"

"I don't like to listen to tapes."

To be happy in retirement, one does not need a lot of "things." Enjoyment can be found in many simple activities. Reading, gardening—even cooking. One senior citizen cooks a favorite dish, enough to feed six persons. She invites five neighbors to her apartment

With meager income, anxiety tarnishes golden years

once a week for the meal. In turn, the other five cook their favorite recipes and invite her.

"It passes time," she beams. "We don't have to be by ourselves. At least we have the evenings when we can all get together for a little fun."

Fourth, *why not borrow a grandchild?* Even if you have some of your own this would be an exciting way to serve your community, church or some busy mother.

Fifth, *plan ahead.* One of the real problems facing many retiring couples is insufficient funds. Recently I heard about a man on a talk show who had planned to retire for many years on a hundred dollars a week. To his bewilderment, he discovered it will take two hundred a week. With inflation, he's facing the future with anxiety. How can he live leisurely with that kind of stress?

Years ago when the individual began planning for his retirement, a hundred dollars a week would have provided a good standard of living. Meanwhile his property taxes quadrupled, food sky-rocketed, clothing prices soared and generally the cost of living jumped year after year.

Instead of looking forward to a life of leisure, many golden couples live on the brink of economic disaster, fearing they will become a burden to their children. Perhaps retirement can be the beginning of life with efficient estate planning and careful management of money.

Free time is intended for relaxation, not worry.

An outing with friends turns leisure into living

You should be able to do the things you want. When I retire, I hope to travel to an uninhabited tropical island, read a lot of books, perhaps spend time at the North Pole or fly on the space shuttle. In fact, if they build a city in space, I'd like to start a church there.

Productive Leisure

Do you find yourself bored, listless and feeling worthless during leisure or retirement? Here are some helpful hints to make your spare hours meaningful:[6]

First, *face your boredom.* Determine to do something about it. Much of the problem results from an inward focus. Preoccupation with boredom leads to further boredom. Instead, make commitments to others, expanding your range of interests and relationships. Challenges are ever present for those who seek them.

Second, *allow yourself to daydream.* When your mind is able to "free-wheel," creativity is stimulated. True interests are revealed, and your inner dimensions of excitement become apparent.

Third, *honor the child inside you.* Don't stifle the playfulness we all have. Adults try too hard to be serious, responsible and unemotional. Let yourself have fun. Laugh!

Fourth, *assert your individuality.* When the child inside you and your daydreams tell you what they want, do it. Leave the weight of responsibilities behind for awhile.

Recreation releases tensions of pressured living

Fifth, *keep physically fit.* Shake off your lethargy and exercise daily. Once the blood is flowing, you'll feel better and life will be more exciting. I enjoy walking. A thirty to forty-minute barefoot stroll along the shore with toes digging into the damp, sandy beach can be invigorating.

Leisure is a God-given opportunity for blessing. Involvement with others during those free hours is both relaxing and rewarding.

Mysterious Paradox

An integral part of life, stress is a mysterious paradox. While pressuring executives into heart attacks, bewildering children into ulcers, intimidating students into nervous exhaustion and badgering housewives into frenzied activity, stress produces growth, strength, fulfillment and creative genius in others.

Because of this, Americans are confused. Many have applied psychological defense mechanisms, offered philosophical answers and discovered practical methods for coping with this infamous killer. Some are learning to turn their stress into success.

6

Turn Your Stress Into Success

Calm, relaxed and smiling, Fred Davis sat in the office facing my desk. "Things are a lot different now," he began. "I don't feel so tense anymore."

Still revealing traces of the agony he had been through, Fred's face was incredibly different from when I had visited him at the hospital just two months before.

"My pace is slower," he continued, "and I have quit looking for extra jobs. This means we've had to lower our standard of living a little, but that's okay. Darla doesn't complain anymore about not having enough.

"I guess . . . no, I *know*—I was using work to satisfy her desire for possessions and to get away from her, too. That just wasn't right. I had to face up to the problem. With God and the doctor's help, we've been able to work out our differences and adjust to the change."

Thinking deeply for a moment, Fred put his finger on the real problem. "I didn't realize working like I did was killing me and ruining my relationships with other people. My wife, children, and people at work annoyed me almost all the time. Now I'm getting along great with those at school; with my family, too, because I found out what was bugging me.

"My daughter, Janie, really needs a lot of attention, which I never took time to give. We're even going out on picnics again—our family, I mean. It's something we used to do that I really enjoyed."

At the mention of this happy activity, Fred's beaming face caused me to smile, remembering the suggestion I had given Darla about resuming these activities.

"And Billy—that boy is really bright!" he continued, leaning forward with palms resting on his knees. "I didn't know Darla and I could raise such a smart kid. Well, anyway, he's helping out a lot, paying for his school expenses at a part-time job."

Fred's face turned sober for a moment as he sat back. "You know, Pastor, I know now that I was really depriving Billy of the chance to prove himself as a . . . well . . . grown-up man. Giving him everything he wanted was wrong. He wanted to learn how to be strong on his own so he might survive in the world out there."

Brightening again, he continued, "You know what? I've taken over Billy's old chore of keeping up the yards and garden. It's really a help to me—makes me slow down and let myself catch up. Using my hands, tending the plants, and the responsibility for their care helps get my mind off work and problems."

The conversation turned to some of the lessons he had learned. "The doctor at the Counseling Clinic told me a lot of things that really made sense. He explained why I worked so hard: I wanted to be worth something to somebody. I thought that would make my family need me more, but instead it drove them away. That's why I, uh, broke down the way I did. It was frustration."

Fred's is just one of the "success from stress" stories I've encountered over the years. Countless times, God has taken broken, stress-filled lives and transformed them into something beautiful and whole.

Accept Yourself

Imagery drives some to attain certain identities that are important to them. Sometimes we are our worst critics and demand unreasonable accomplishments from ourselves.

God made you just as you are. He not only gave you your physical features, but your temperament. Most individuals under stress have difficulty accepting themselves. Perfectionists tend to set unattainable goals. Make certain that you are first following God's designs for your life.

If you are better equipped and skilled to be a farmer, a mechanic or a construction worker, don't pressure yourself with an ambition to be a doctor, a scientist or a professor.

Authorities point out that we have produced a generation that is over-educated but underskilled. Every occupation has dignity.

Accept Your Limitations

Every person has a load limit. I believe we should examine our lives from a practical standpoint, emerging triumphantly from self-imposed pressures. If you're under stress, ask yourself: "What am I trying to hold onto that I feel I may lose?" By limiting our battles to those we can realistically expect to handle, we can conquer stress and force frustration to flee.

Our attitude often determines the amount of stress we encounter. Borrowing a page from theology, we can say that people have either a "law" model—harshly judging themselves in terms of performance—or a "grace" model—one of self-acceptance.

Those under the law are tormented by stress because they never measure up to the standards they set. But under the acceptance model of grace, we are in touch with our "smallness" and reach up to God for help. Grace enters when we realize that God accepts us in spite of our weakness. Amazingly, God searches for us in our frailty to supply this grace.

Applying the grace model in a psychological and spiritual context, we need not fear the trauma of stress, nor push ourselves past our limits. When anxiety does arrive, we can relieve it by drawing close to God.

"In my distress I cried unto the Lord, and he heard me," King David wrote. "I will both lay me down in peace, and sleep: for thou, Lord, only makest me dwell in safety."[1]

Perspectives on Pressure

People perceive the same pressures differently, depending on their perspective. As the Bible relates the story, Elisha and his servant were surrounded by the military hordes of Syria, but Elisha stood cool, calm and collected. His aide, on the other hand, was suffering an anxiety attack! Involved in the same crisis, they had completely different attitudes: Elisha was confident of God's protection while the servant moaned, "Oh no, I've had it now!"

Praying that his servant's eyes would be opened to see God's protection, Elisha smiled as the aide gasped in surprise; they were surrounded by a spiritual army of horses and fiery chariots! Knowing God is on your side is an astounding antidote to anxiety.[2]

How do we develop this "grace-full" attitude toward stress? The Bible again supplies a perfect example.[3] Facing imminent invasion of his country by the massing armies of the Moabites, Ammonites and Edomites, King Jehosaphat turned to God in his plight:

> Oh Lord God of our fathers—the only God in all the heavens, the Ruler of all the kingdoms of the earth—you are so powerful, so mighty. Who can stand against you?

Notice that Jehosaphat didn't panic. He began praising God for who He is, the source of all power and the one with the final say among the nations of the Earth.

> Oh our God, didn't you drive out the heathen who lived in this land. . . ., (giving it) forever to the descendants of your friend Abraham?

He kept praising God for what He had already done. If God gave the land to Israel, He surely could be expected to protect it. Jehosaphat demonstrated his confidence that their continued presence in the land was God's will.

> Your people settled here and built this Temple for you, truly believing that in a time like this . . . we can stand here before (it) . . . and cry out to you to save us. . . .

The king professed his relationship to God, expressing confidence that He would not fail His own people. Finally pointing out the problem at hand, Jehosaphat made his request, knowing that God would accept it despite the people's failings:

> Now see what the armies . . . are doing. . . . They have come to throw us out of your land which you have given us. O our God, won't you stop them? We have no way to protect ourselves against this mighty army. We don't know what to do, but we are looking to you.

In response to this plea of submission and confidence, God promised victory. "Don't be afraid," He told them, "for the battle is not yours, but God's!"

The Battle is God's

If only we recognize this incredible insight: all our battles are God's. Harmful stress results from fighting in our own strength on too many fronts at once. Surrendering our anxieties to God will lift much of the burden we feel.

When stress strikes, here are three simple steps to keep the pressures in perspective.

First, *recognize the purpose of the crisis*. Ask God, "What are you trying to teach me?" This doesn't mean that every time you are in a crisis you have done something wrong. Many lessons in life come through perplexing circumstances, and God sometimes speaks to us very plainly through these difficult experiences.

Second, *see God's solution* to your difficulty, however stressful it may be. Don't panic; give God time, and think it through.

Third, *praise God* that you are already on the way out. Though the armies of anxiety surround you, know that deliverance is coming. If you are a friend of Jesus Christ, your position is absolutely secure!

Stress From Success

Some neglect these divine principles and reverse the delights of success into stress. Having been blessed of God through dependence on Him, they now say: "Thanks for the ride, God. I'll take it from here."

A woman called me recently, tearfully reporting problems in her marriage. "Pastor, I just don't understand it! My husband has dropped out of church, and he's not interested in spiritual things anymore." When I asked why, she thought for a moment and concluded, "It's because he's succeeded. Because he has it made, he's forgotten God. He feels he doesn't need God anymore."

It is unfortunate that some people cannot be blessed without forgetting God. He wants to prosper your business and still have you maintain your physical, mental and spiritual balance. He's ready to take care of the daily stresses produced by success, but He will not compete with greed.

The Business Battle

One of our deacons at Melodyland relies totally on God despite his success. Working in the garment industry, he faces the squeeze of intense pressure every day, but he has an exciting way to cope with it.

"In my business I have to deal with all kinds of people," he relates, "those who work for me, manufacturers, unions. I make coats, and the working situations aren't always the best. Last year, the manufacturers couldn't decide on the lengths for coats, and the summer was hot. Who needs coats then? To top it off, there was a trucking strike.

"The stores panicked and quit buying coats; the manufacturers had to stop giving us work, and there we sat, watching the competition pouring in from overseas. Here I am in the middle of this, responsible for my workers, foremen and factories. I had to borrow money so my people could get paid. You talk about stress!"

How does he handle the pressure?

"I really have to ask God to guide me. There have been times when I've locked the door to my office, knelt down and opened up the Bible to the Psalms. I've always related to David in the Bible because I seem to think a little bit like him, I guess. In one passage he talked about the oppression of his enemies, and I would sit and actually read the verse to the Lord as if saying, 'Lord, please take over. I can't stand this anymore, and I mean it!' And because I do trust God, I know in my heart that He did take over."

This deacon believes God especially helps him to do the jobs he doesn't enjoy. A person can suffer a great deal of stress forcing himself to complete a project his heart isn't in, but that is when the strength of Jesus comes through in special power.

"Don't get me wrong," he continues. "I love my work. I love the pressure and the things that are difficult to make happen. It's fun to grow through a challenge, like the times when you don't know where the next dollar is coming from and you have the pressure of putting everything together. But I'm glad I've made up my mind to ask God for help.

"Sure, I fall down a lot. Maybe a day will come to an end, and I feel I've failed. But I get on my knees at night and wake up the next morning ready to go again. I keep plunging ahead, and God knows I won't give up because in every situation I encounter I have His security to hold me."

To complicate their potentially stressful lifestyle, the deacon and his wife have another area of tension with which they have had to cope. They come from different religious backgrounds, one a Roman Catholic and the other a Protestant. A potentially explosive combination, this can produce enough stress to wreck any home and leave the family deeply embittered. However, they have found a way to make their relationship succeed.

"I thank God that we have a happy home," he beams. "It hasn't been easy. At the time we were married, a Protestant and Catholic just didn't get married. It's rough, and we've had our trying times, but it's getting easier."

Pondering this, his wife counsels, "I don't recommend mixed marriages. I think that we have worked this out because Christ is the Head of our home. If you can put Him first, the other things will follow. Without Christ, it just won't work."

The husband agrees. "There are a lot of things a person says when he's upset and under stress, things that he doesn't really mean. At times I'd bring up the history of the Catholic church, then feel a check inside of me that says, 'You know something? She loves the same God you do and serves the same Jesus you do.'

"I fell in love with her right away, but with my religious background, I also believed Catholics weren't supposed to make it to Heaven. It was hard to adjust to her not eating meat on Friday, covering her head

*Catholic-Protestant intermarriage
has been turned into family happiness*

when we went to church and never missing Mass because she thought it would be a sin. I guess it was because we both really love Jesus and love each other very much that it began to work out."

"There were times when he wasn't too kind," she reflects. "I really felt hurt and rejected sometimes, as if he thought I loved the church more than him, or something. But because I love Jesus and I know he does too, I wanted to show my husband that he is the first in my life—after God, of course."

Stress Into Success

The stress of life cannot be avoided, but it can be turned into success with God's help.

With God's power and a balanced lifestyle, the strains of life cannot only be managed but turned into a positive force for creativity. Free from the weariness and disease that pressure often brings, we can have a happy family life, a satisfying occupation and turn our stresses into success.

Today I told our prayer group of several thousand, which meets on Thursday mornings, that I don't have problems. God has them because He has me, and if He has me, He has the responsibility for those problems.

One day He spoke to my heart while I was carrying a burden: "Are you going to worry about that problem, or are you going to let me? I'm a lot better equipped to handle it than you."

God will not worry about something if you're going to. This is the guiding principle of my life.

Turn Your Stress Into Success

Every time I've been under stress, I've looked for success in it.

Footnotes

Chapter 1

[1]Hans Selye, *Stress Without Distress* (Signet Books, J. B. Lippincot Co., New York, 1974), pp. 14, 15, 18, 19.

[2]Gary Collins, *You Can Profit From Stress* (Vision House, Santa Ana, Calif., 1977), pp. 13, 14.

[3]Job 1:21.

[4]II Cor. 4:8, 9, 17 (Living Bible).

[5]Collins, *op. cit.*, pp. 22, 23.

Chapter 2

[1]Fred Davis is a fictional character based in part on the real life case of an individual counseled at Melodyland. His problems represent a cross section of pressures faced by many in similar situations. The name of his high school also has been changed to further protect his identity.

[2]James J. Lynch, *The Broken Heart* (Basic Books, New York, 1977), p. 100.

[3]Dr. O. Carl Simonton, M.D., "Management of the Emotional Aspects of Malignancy," a lecture given June 14 and 15, 1974 at the University of Florida.

[4]*Ibid.*

[5]Quoted in Collins, *op. cit.*, p. 28. Other sources: Paul Martin, "How to Rid Yourself of Tension," *Let's LIVE*, March 1978, p. 30; Richard Gore, "Stress and How to Help Him Cope With It," *Harper's Bazaar*, October 1976, p. 56.

[6]Wayne E. Oates, *Confessions of a Workaholic* (Abingdon Press, Nashville, Tenn., 1971), p. 13.

[7]Matt. 5:48.

[8]Alvin Toffler, *Future Shock* (Random House, New York, 1970), pp. 324, 325.

[9]Matt. 6:34 *(Living Bible)*.

[10]J. B. Phillips, *Your God Is Too Small* (Macmillan Publishing Co., New York, 1961), pp. 55, 56.

Chapter 3

[1]Dr. Robert C. Page, *How to Lick Executive Stress* (Cornerstone Library, New York, 1961), pp. 131, 132.

[2]Bud Gordon, "Women Who Have Full-Time Jobs and Run Homes Face Illness From Stress," *National Enquirer*, Feb. 21, 1978, p. 29.

[3]Larry Christenson, *The Christian Family* (Bethany Fellowship, Minneapolis, Minn., 1970), pp. 11, 12.

[4]Eph. 5:22-6:4.

Chapter 4

[1]Job 1:21.

[2]Job 1:22.

[3]Prov. 22:6.

[4]Prov. 24:10; Psa. 4:1, II Cor. 12:10.

[5]Dr. Hans Selye as told to Laurence Cherry, "On the Real Benefits of Distress," *Psychology Today*, March 1978, pp. 60, 63.

[6]"Cracking Under Stress," *U.S. News and World Report*, May 20, 1976, p. 60.

Gen. 2:2.

[8]Mark 6:31.

[9]Matt. 6:34.

[10]Selye and Cherry, *op. cit.*, p. 70.

[11]Rollo May, ed., *Existential Psychology* (Random House, New York, 1960).

[12]John 14:6.

[13]Phil. 4:7.

[14]Isa. 30:15.

[15]Matt. 6:25; Phil. 4:6.

[16]Rom. 14:17.

Chapter 5

[1]"How Americans Pursue Happiness," *U.S. News and World Report*, May 23, 1977, p. 63.

[2]Alexander Reid Martin, "Leisure and Our Inner Resources," *Parks and Recreation*, March 1975, p. 4a.

[3]*Ibid.*, p. 3a.

[4]Dwight F. Rettie, "A New Perspective on Leisure," *Parks and Recreation*, August 1974, p. 25.

[5]"Leisure Spending Defies the Recession," *Business Week*, April 14, 1975, p. 22.

[6]Based on a list by James Lincoln Collier, "Leisure—Why Don't We Enjoy It More?" *Reader's Digest*, July 1973, pp. 167, 168.

Chapter 6

[1]Psa. 120:1; 4:8.

[2]II Kings 6:15-17.

[3]II Chron. 20:6-12, 15 *(Living Bible)*.

Notes

Notes

Notes

Notes

Notes

Notes

Notes